Copyright © Dianne Cikusa 2020

The moral right of the author has been asserted in accordance with the Copyright Amendment (Moral Rights) Act 2000.

All rights reserved. Except as permitted under the Australian Copyright Act 1968 (for example, fair dealing for the purposes of study, research, criticism or review) no part of this publication may be reproduced, stored in a retrieval system, or transmitted in any form or by any means, electronic, mechanical, photocopying, recording or otherwise, without the written permission of the publisher.

Cataloguing-in-Publication entry is available from the National Library of Australia: http://catalogue.nla.gov.au/

Title:	The Little Tree of Wisdom
Subtitle:	365 Insights
Author:	Cikusa, Dianne, 1973–
ISBNs:	978-0-6484923-6-8 (paperback)
Subjects:	BODY, MIND & SPIRIT: Inspiration & Personal Growth; PHILOSOPHY: Mind & Body; SELF-HELP: Motivational & Inspirational; Personal Growth / General

Cover and internal images under license from Adobe Stock

Cover design by Ally Mosher @ allymosher.com

Published by Mignon Press, 2020

PO Box 922, Katoomba NSW 2780

mignon
PRESS

Books by Dianne Cikusa:

Hope and Substance

The Sea In-Between

The Rain Sermon: Le Sermon de la Pluie

Who saw Beauty cry, and forgot to hold her left hand?: Meditations for women

The Jigsaw of Eight Thousand Pieces: Soul Reflections

The Little Tree of Wisdom: 365 Insights

Ocho plumas de un pájaro muerto
(Español)

Ocho plumas sin vuelo ni eternidad
huérfanas de pájaro caído
al jugoso mordisco de la huerta.
Ocho plumas del aire
 aterrizan en la muerte del sabor
de aquella naranja comida en la mirada
del pájaro devorado por las circunstancias.

Caer como si fuéramos amanecer triste
hundiéndonos tierra adentro
raíz de alas felices que fuimos en vuelo.

                                              Juan Garrido-Salgado

Eight feathers of a dead bird
(English)

Eight feathers without eternity or flight
orphaned birds fallen
to the juicy bite of the garden.
Eight feathers of the air
 they land in the death of taste
of that orange eaten by the gaze
of the bird devoured by circumstances.

Falling like we're sad dawn
sinking inland
root of happy wings that went in flight.

Juan Garrido-Salgado

Insight #1

How many times have you walked to Heaven up the wrong stairs?

Insight #2

There is only so far that a 'spiritual hand' can guide a stubborn mind.

Insight #3

Nobody wins, and everybody wins nothing.

Insight #4

Life passes rapidly [whilst speaking].

Insight #5

Strong pride makes for an independent fool.

Insight #6

Idyllic love -- is all of our glamorous projection.

Insight #7

Push personal opinion harder, for ever-less response.

Insight #8

Without drama, we all have precious little to say.

Insight #9

The heavyweight champion is the one who knows he will never conquer gravity.

Insight #10

One's level of awareness relates directly to one's understanding of death.

Insight #11

In exaggerating proportion, we cleverly drew out irrelevance.

Insight #12

Death keeps repeating, what we don't like to be noticing.

Insight #13

Ego is every victim.

Insight #14

When you crumble, you humble.

Insight #15

Perfect thoughts are empty.

Insight #16

There are only two facts of life:
Death and Volition

Insight #17

Where we couldn't deal with our terror, we faced desire.

Insight #18

Beauty is having a leg;
Joy is having a life.

Insight #19

Death will devour the mind in small pieces: dollar by subtle dollar [and inconspicuous cent].

Insight #20

Your judgement is your brutal truth in this moment.

Insight #21

I won't end up like my parents;
how did I end up as my parents?

Insight #22

There is no good life, just God life.

Insight #23

Overt pride is lacking the courage to demonstrate a vulnerable face.

Insight #24

Why, why, why -- do we all keep rehearsing the same ways?

Insight #25

Fear assumes many names [... all of them starting with 'death'].

Insight #26

Don't blame the chair -- you sat in it.

Insight #27

While soul-play observes, the mind-play has already begun reacting.

Insight #28

Denial follows, wherever the trail of addiction leads.

Insight #29

God is the Poem for which it takes an eternity to earn resplendent meaning.

Insight #30

Destiny is only as fluid as one's knowledge of the ocean.

Insight #31

Compassion esteems love in reverse.

Insight #32

Perception repeats old intelligence.

Insight #33

Mind thinks itself enlightened [... until the emotions rush in to argue].

Insight #34

Death is just a covert attitude to Life.

Insight #35

Does your ego know how to eloquently take the joke of its own life?

Insight #36

If it means 'nothing', then there is no overriding inclination to prove its validity.

Insight #37

A conscious moon... does all the pulling and pushing.

Insight #38

Death is within, without, around, through -- and beyond.

Insight #39

Society taught us to open our minds (and so we hardly stopped closing our mouths).

Insight #40

The answer aligns with the Self, but a question stays faithful to all.

Insight #41

Will you still be comparing characteristics at somebody's funeral?

Insight #42

Love is refined by the diligence of everyone's diplomacy.

Insight #43

'Confidence' is significantly believing in one's personal identity.

Insight #44

Child will only be as 'special' as the parents make him feel.

Insight #45

Don't blame movement where you couldn't slow down your impatience.

Insight #46

To God, we all look cute.

Insight #47

How does one present 'death' to the

language of Fear?

Insight #48

What is misaligned is smugly misinterpreted by the mind.

Insight #49

Everyone is interested if it pertains to their own desire.

Insight #50

Some relationships may ask obtrusively to be granted reimbursements.

Insight #51

Where we choose to behave as animals, we may die like bloodied beasts.

Insight #52

Life is both a determined and a creative effort.

Insight #53

Relax. Life can happen to anyone.

Insight #54

There is absolutely nothing to prove in the end, just as there is no absolute proof of faith at the beginning.

Insight #55

Handfuls of ignored pain... successively add up.

Insight #56

Words don't make us sick, indulgent energy does.

Insight #57

Only 'stillness' is justice.

Insight #58

Universal energy transmits via our humanitarian satellite.

Insight #59

Lifetimes sit ahead;
Wisdom rests impeccably behind.

Insight #60

Where a perception of wealth is larger than your own, the 'I' must have it.

Insight #61

Guilt has happened;
Judgement requires now to process it.

Insight #62

Hoping that death won't happen, won't work back avoidance.

Insight #63

Teach the body so the head can likewise understand.

Insight #64

You can't insult the ocean by fire.

Insight #65

Words might not make up the entirety of an apology, but a restorative action will.

Insight #66

Wise essence -- said it once only.

Insight #67

Notwithstanding a certain death,
there is really no problem.

Insight #68

Enlightenment is a conscious body less a dense mind.

Insight #69

Every thought sticks out, while it waits furtively to catch you up.

Insight #70

You mightn't call it by a jealous name,
but that's what it will be.

Insight #71

Love is not the point, but rather the focused line.

Insight #72

Compassion shrinks the stomach;
Faith empties the mind.

Insight #73

Conversations leave out frequent words: death [and death].

Insight #74

Boring defines as... someone stuck rigidly to the sentiment of themselves.

Insight #75

How much egocentricity did you wake up with this morning?
[Roll over those emotional cadavers, hour by dissipating hour].

Insight #76

Rage runs on batteries; spirit-heart connects ardently at the source.

Insight #77

Judgement can't see through a blizzard; Guilt just eats the snow.

Insight #78

Our feminine heart dreams of forever. Our masculine mind is happy while it lasts.

Insight #79

Body image is made in God's image.

Insight #80

Living awareness -- sees the quicker second upfront.

Insight #81

Spirit makes and [teasingly] breaks with our self-assurance.

Insight #82

Nothing more than basic faith is lacking.

Insight #83

It's not that men and women don't understand each other, but that unenlightened men and women won't understand each other.

Insight #84

How many 'spirit eggs' can you fit into your one basket of truth?

Insight #85

Death is the unconditional reality,
so why do we keep denying it?

Insight #86

Did you know... you were only ever speaking about yourself?

Insight #87

Water was only heavy where we tried to contain it.

Insight #88

Fingers stain with the blood of haughty forgiveness.

Insight #89

Life will not always be the way your self-importance wants it.

Insight #90

Love is a sphere;

awareness is the whirlpool.

Insight #91

Surrender is both mundane -- and exhilarating.

Insight #92

A tempered face reflects in the hearth of Spirit.

Insight #93

We each feed our own mentality to believe that another will die first.

Insight #94

Making a living is simultaneously making its death.

Insight #95

A 'sexualised' product sells overboard to the passionate consumer.

Insight #96

The flowers of 'spiritual ecstasy' grow up from the soils of one's cultivated perception.

Insight #97

Spirit laughs at what it once <u>was</u>. Ego laughs at what it cannot see it still <u>is</u>.

Insight #98

Superiority speaks too loudly, and for too long.

Insight #99

Happiness springs from the juvenile mind; Joy stems from a wise heart.

Insight #100

'Abundance' does not undertake to bulldoze the mindset of inner poverty.

Insight #101

Real magic is something more than zealous entertainment.

Insight #102

Awareness has stocked the shelf;
Ignorance was only stockpiling.

Insight #103

When the Higher life comes together... Resentment bolts, and Guilt locks the door behind itself.

Insight #104

Change is always offending somebody.

Insight #105

Private property: We only think and think to own it.

Insight #106

Inner Time is the revitalising balance

of all our energy-in-motion.

Insight #107

Get a dynamic grip on death, not life.

Insight #108

The first thing we do by emotional fire is PANIC.

Insight #109

Every day is <u>somebody's</u> last day on earth.

Insight #110

Too many people have too much to say about God.

Insight #111

Prove nothing, to no-one who cares.
Prove your body, to itself only.

Insight #112

Ego seeks to fill ideals,
seldom to fulfill Higher ones.

Insight #113

Needs change, along with our progressing consciousness.

Insight #114

The artificial high stands to lose more ground.

Insight #115

You asked for prodding by the devil's fork.

Insight #116

Shake death... to see again your perception of 'alive'.

Insight #117

Mind will judge the technique;
Soul will guide around its process.

Insight #118

When the pain wears off, you will be reminded to laugh.

Insight #119

Prayer *proposes* to live in God's love;
Faith acts on behalf of that prayer.

Insight #120

The place of beauty is the space between two hearts.

Insight #121

God owes us no grand explanations;
neither does our spirit.

Insight #122

The trip of a lifetime... is by now speedily going.

Insight #123

Authenticity waits until an intoxicated ego wears off.

Insight #124

Resentment is deaf and blindly dumb.

Insight #125

'Sadness' reverts back to the death of old control.

Insight #126

When the rain stops falling, essence is current.

Insight #127

The personality represents a single stream, whereas Soul is inclusive of the ocean.

Insight #128

Life is comparable only by joy.

Insight #129

All we need to cast a beneficial spell --

is a rhyme.

Insight #130

Compassion is on serene terms with the body's emotional energy.

Insight #131

Where is your 'thinking' going, with attachment proudly by its side?

Insight #132

Wheresoever the fear is unconscious,
reality is staying the same.

Insight #133

Success measures by how far we have come <u>into</u> the work of our faith.

Insight #134

Where we could not willingly cry, we laughed instead.

Insight #135

A gentle soul is a gentle-sounding personality.

Insight #136

Take your breath seriously, not your words.

Insight #137

Ego has interest only of the act,
Spirit of the acting essence.

Insight #138

When you become master of your own body, it is then you will have something actual to say.

Insight #139

Gratitude is the art of simplified approval.

Insight #140

Emotional pain -- has only its slice of affection to blame.

Insight #141

Soul watches, even behind the eyes of an occupant child.

Insight #142

God loves a sinner who laughs first,

and then repents.

Insight #143

So long as someone *else* dies, <u>we</u> are seeming safer.

Insight #144

When it comes to a divine 'nothing',
you've succeeded.

Insight #145

Spirit gathers the sticks to make conscious the fire.

Insight #146

The hardest battle is beating your hating heart.

Insight #147

A love of possessiveness is the grapplehook of emotional control.

Insight #148

To our clinging mind, life is a killer.

Insight #149

Higher awareness has lesser need to yield itself to a human bargain.

Insight #150

Though it's a man's world, boy cried his way into it.

Insight #151

Ego fears a bad life, and a painful death.

Insight #152

Sex isn't free. Sex is <u>never</u> free.

Insight #153

Don't hold the clown to a solemn question.

Insight #154

When you stop having fun, then you'll think of God.

Insight #155

'Conditional love' is a fearful distortion of our free will.

Insight #156

Observe the passing signs of an unfolding moment.

Insight #157

Questions are answered by death's muted doorknock.

Insight #158

Pick up the heaviest emotional suitcase [it's probably yours].

Insight #159

Life is about the *consciousness* behind the consumption.

Insight #160

Time didn't fly; our ego just slipped by unnoticed.

Insight #161

Delusion measures the length and width of our mortal desires.

Insight #162

Will you retain the moisture, or will you keep adding judgement?

Insight #163

Gold is the colour of one's acquisitive hands, feet and tongue.

Insight #164

If your superiority is so smart, then why are you struggling?

Insight #165

Ignorance grows back.

Insight #166

Two shallow ends have no concept of death.

Insight #167

Though small gains were made, was any lesson actually l-earned?

Insight #168

'Wisdom' was often hastily interviewed and coldly retrenched.

Insight #169

Presence picks a winning horse in every running moment.

Insight #170

Where do we each begin, to hold the venerable energy of our soul?

Insight #171

Be gentle with the staples in my mind [... the heart might readily split again].

Insight #172

The pool of Higher wisdom... is an emotional loop.

Insight #173

Spirits have the wisest intention;
minds hold only a supreme motive.

Insight #174

Keep both the humour and sensitivity in balance [to endure alongside of any jealousy and competing judgement].

Insight #175

How much arrogant head space is your body taking up?

Insight #176

Joy gets <u>inside</u> every requirement;
poverty grabs at the space.

Insight #177

Where two won't equally unite, there may split three.

Insight #178

Life expends [with or without a conscious soul].

Insight #179

Death allows you this day --
don't beat down the door.

Insight #180

Yang is generating a world.

Yin is sustaining it.

Insight #181

When the 'energy' has finished with you, movement will take it away.

Insight #182

Something is only as good as its discernible Essence.

Insight #183

How much inadvertent emotion have you stored behind the delusion?

Insight #184

What is your ego [sincerely] doing for humanity?

Insight #185

Self-awareness articulates a Higher relationship to the past.

Insight #186

Enlightenment has metaphorically slept with the 'other side' of Self.

Insight #187

Life is passing... no matter what you do.

Insight #188

If you think it, reality will likely harvest it.

Insight #189

Your life happened, so you reacted to it.

Insight #190

Thin mental lines systematically crossed out a thick emotional past.

Insight #191

That humble appointment with patience: Sorry, we missed it.

Insight #192

It's a humanity thing, so leave man & woman out of it.

Insight #193

You can play the mind game, but does body know what it's all about?

Insight #194

Life takes its chances at the improbability of death.

Insight #195

The young dream believes to tell the world.

Insight #196

When hopes are smashed, personality looks in another bottle.

Insight #197

Death is always closer in energy, than in years.

Insight #198

Karmic debt pays daily into the human purse of ignorance.

Insight #199

Youth lays bare the parental hopes.

Insight #200

Deals with the devil may later attempt to make accords with God.

Insight #201

When life is reduced to nil, it will then show its true internal value.

Insight #202

The spirit-mind is ineffably wise;
the ego-mind is doubtless trying.

Insight #203

Our add-ons... are guardedly following us everywhere.

Insight #204

Empathy sees to the depth;
sympathy looks only on the surface.

Insight #205

World catches up to the believer.

Insight #206

Let go! Even 1% anger may compound frustrated interest.

Insight #207

Taking all one's evolving behaviour into account, this life *is* the next life.

Insight #208

Body energy speaks words that lips have coolly sealed.

Insight #209

Any upheld fantasy will only drive an image closer to its essence.

Insight #210

Wake up their 'inner eye' by loudest whisper.

Insight #211

Self-awareness can hit upon the cure for any-thing.

Insight #212

How much implicit energy, sparks between you and your world aspiration?

Insight #213

Every depression has need of an outward expression.

Insight #214

Prettiness -- is perhaps a little more face.

Insight #215

When the awe wears off, jealousy sets in.

Insight #216

We all started somewhere... and unintentionally ended up someplace else.

Insight #217

Hatred is a coarse energy that hasn't yet found its spiritual way home.

Insight #218

What does your blessed head think...
to be achieving for the greater plight
of humanity?

Insight #219

Even though Spirit is giving us true joy, <u>we</u> kept stealing after pleasure.

Insight #220

Inadequately addressed emotions may attract newfound reservations.

Insight #221

We sell off global power;
we buy back eternal soul.

Insight #222

Wake up from the reverie of your illusory emotion.

Insight #223

Some people's lives take up all the room in other people's heads.

Insight #224

Pink is the commemorative colour of our watered-down blood.

Insight #225

Well, of course things look different to the other way of reality!

Insight #226

Life <u>depends</u> on us each coming down to earth.

Insight #227

Beliefs are often cumbersome where the standpoint is shallow.

Insight #228

Creativity is all the magnificently dressed-up colour of brown.

Insight #229

Ego writes as the attention sees.

Insight #230

Size weighs more to the mind.

Insight #231

Demand yet another promise of safety, but only for the future of desire.

Insight #232

You weren't reading the soul transcript, but rather its egoistic translation.

Insight #233

Move on... but from what, and to whom?

Insight #234

Whose emergency is making you out to look a hero?

Insight #235

wherever the cursor is, finds my denial.

Insight #236

It is all of that revolving 'e-motion', which keeps us habitually alive.

Insight #237

'Creating' came from essential pain.

Insight #238

Life's perpetual marking pen won't always stop to make allowances for our misguided feelings.

Insight #239

You are effectively buying the <u>person</u> behind the product.

Insight #240

Unity is arduously bathed in diverse reactions.

Insight #241

Emotion... is really going in no direction.

Insight #242

The little success thought it won forever.

Insight #243

'Belief' is all of our invested illusion.

Insight #244

Money earns by the human hour;
Soul earns by refreshing deed.

Insight #245

Surrealism is abstract opinion.

Insight #246

'Time' simply tracks the movement of our deviating energy.

Insight #247

Compassion = Detachment
(of the wisest kind)

Insight #248

God picked up the tab wherever we picked upon the tabloid.

Insight #249

Essence is subtracted from what you think you know.

Insight #250

'Tolerance' is the mirror of our polished judgement.

Insight #251

The answer is both true <u>and</u> false.

Insight #252

Speech is itself an impediment.

Insight #253

Where you ordered the menu, it's yours to wholly consume.

Insight #254

Body is the visible mind of consumption.

Insight #255

Slow down the human clock, seamlessly turn back the spirit consciousness.

Insight #256

Delusion is first emotional, then physical.

Insight #257

Dreams -- open up the sky of consciousness.

Insight #258

Death is a daily wakefulness, not an annual visit to the cemetery.

Insight #259

True compassion respects and releases the ego-mind in others.

Insight #260

What body says, lazy does.

Insight #261

Since man is not God and woman is no angel, we will all somewhere have to make compromise.

Insight #262

What kind of 'sex object' did you envision yourself to be?

Insight #263

Death marks the pages to a presumptuous life.

Insight #264

A supportive heart credits the tiniest thing (and forgives the largest piece).

Insight #265

Since you've already lost the game,
start again smiling.

Insight #266

As love fails, time spends.

Insight #267

Knowledge ends on a full stop;
Wisdom leaves behind a comma.

Insight #268

Material life lives outside of the consciousness.

Insight #269

Human vices are re-absorbed by the plenitude of newer distractions.

Insight #270

What you despise in *this* life, could certainly become you in the next.

Insight #271

Judgement day is every Sunday.

Insight #272

Soul makes aware the infinite yearning;
Life settles the finite debt.

Insight #273

Justice involves other people;
Karma concerns myself only.

Insight #274

Life regrets its [inescapable] death.

Insight #275

Energy invests time into the liquefying years.

Insight #276

Poverty is the unkind look on your face.

Insight #277

Loving fills an empty space;
Love *is* the empty space.

Insight #278

Buddhas don't make in one day.

Insight #279

Find your money something healthier to do.

Insight #280

More and more past life is flashing before your eyes.

Insight #281

Time is a perpetuating engagement with our multi-dimensional self.

Insight #282

It's not real, until it's death all over.

Insight #283

Ego quantity substitutes for spirit quality.

Insight #284

Impatience is slow to accept the attendance of everyday reality.

Insight #285

Life happens, until we learn to diffuse the burgeoning input of fate.

Insight #286

A mother inherently risks that her children become more powerful.

Insight #287

If it gets into undesirable hands, it may be seen by indecorous eyes.

Insight #288

Listen closely to what falls out of the intellectual mouth.

Insight #289

Birth is our first-again contact with 'physical' karma.

Insight #290

If beauty excludes, then maybe it wasn't beauty.

Insight #291

The person whom you cannot easily forgive, is your imperfect self.

Insight #292

Nobody believes all of what you say, save for the merit of themselves.

Insight #293

Death makes no excuses;

People do.

Insight #294

Pushy advertising is sometimes stating above the product.

Insight #295

Ego is more often than not blind,
though God is not.

Insight #296

You may come to hate as you once loved, and fear as you first thought to laugh.

Insight #297

Collect venom from every snake that bit you.

Insight #298

I am not who you think I am --
I am not you!

Insight #299

Watch your subliminal home movies for some altruistic insights.

Insight #300

Delusion makes us happy;
Reality makes us wise.

Insight #301

You are not a human body, but rather a human-living 'soul'.

Insight #302

Death seems a big thing to a little ego.

Insight #303

'Grasping' love... is ever-so-ready to fall into trap again.

Insight #304

Who has kindly found their way into your childhood heart?

Insight #305

Do not force by words what is best absorbed by personal experience.

Insight #306

Age in itself, reveals nothing about the soul's enlightenment.

Insight #307

Ego is a matter of physical fact.

Insight #308

Unhappiness... is very much longing for perfected connection.

Insight #309

Friends are how many you add, subtract and divide among them.

Insight #310

Resentment isn't new, but is renewed by resuscitating forces.

Insight #311

When there is no humility, there is no resultant compassion.

Insight #312

<u>Live</u> as angel;
don't just believe in one.

Insight #313

Death has a quietly reverberating effect.

Insight #314

Cancer -- is everybody's emotional problem.

Insight #315

We often believe in a dream, but may fail to work through to its pertinent reality.

Insight #316

How many times did you 'inwardly'
meet with your death today?

Insight #317

Argue the point,... until the point loses direction.

Insight #318

The World is actively spoken about;
The Universe is passively observed.

Insight #319

Time inevitably heals all perceptible wounds and exposes every naked lie.

Insight #320

Our human path... is self-cleaning of emotion.

Insight #321

The 'game' is between the ladies; man has only one motive.

Insight #322

While man expects a return, woman prefers a secure deposit.

Insight #323

Where a body energy firmly says 'no', you will have little chance to defeat it.

Insight #324

Female is an intuitive guide to love;
Male is a natural channel for sex.

Insight #325

Everything will die, but ignorance will kill it faster.

Insight #326

Only karma lies beyond the stratosphere.

Insight #327

Shrink that discordant emotional tumour, before it has a chance to grow past the hemispheres of mind.

Insight #328

There is no feasible God, just an ever-circulating universal energy.

Insight #329

Time is but death seen in passing.

Insight #330

Animosity declines to accept the other as its spiritual equal.

Insight #331

Every 'unconscious' action as likely meets with an equally oppositional <u>re</u>action.

Insight #332

Beyond a point of concrete awareness,
life is no better for owning more.

Insight #333

Someone else already suffered a part of your life in advance [and dynamically paved the road behind them].

Insight #334

Physically, we can't digest all memory at once.

Insight #335

Body is a block of wood, Spirit is the commissioned carver.

Insight #336

Life seems fairly straightforward
[until we hit into a wall].

Insight #337

Thinking -- is talking in currency.

Insight #338

Death is a highly-civilised question: Why then, does nobody wish to answer it?

Insight #339

The more that people are earth-bound, the heavier becomes heaven.

Insight #340

Your acceptance is undoubtedly another's rejection.

Insight #341

Competition and craving -- always trim down to attachment and pain.

Insight #342

Learn to separate real suffering from whomever is pining for an extra treat.

Insight #343

whose sex, should pay the extra dollar?

Insight #344

Somewhere along the karmic line, you too were making a circuitous contribution.

Insight #345

De-composure is the other half of God.

Insight #346

Shrink death, until it walks by your level side.

Insight #347

The toxins of consumption are cleansed by pure deliberation only.

Insight #348

Say nothing [calmly].

Insight #349

Where pain is misunderstood, the cure will remain unheard.

Insight #350

Power comes... when the body learns to believe its own death.

Insight #351

Compassion lowers envy to zero.

Insight #352

'Detachment' is devoid of all entrenched superiority.

Insight #353

You're not my soul to tell.

Insight #354

Best friends are interconnected spirits.

Insight #355

What are you *doing* for money?
What are you *being* for peace?

Insight #356

Keeping wise is a full-time occupation.

Insight #357

Enlightenment is exemplified by the status of 'well-being over time'.

Insight #358

Who's been crudely stuffing spam down Santa's letterbox?

Insight #359

Aloneness is an impossible triumph.

Insight #360

Judgement parts the 'whole' love.

Insight #361

Positive role reversal:

Father teaches you to love yourself; Mother teaches you never to be afraid of anything.

Insight #362

Life understands -- from a bigger kid point of view.

Insight #363

Laughing <u>after</u> the fall is the lesson; laughing <u>during</u> the fall is wisdom.

Insight #364

When enough people cry, God makes more rain.

Insight #365

In the end, everyone has a simple life.

For information please visit:

www.mignonpress.com

www.ingramcontent.com/pod-product-compliance
Lightning Source LLC
Chambersburg PA
CBHW050259010526
44107CB00055B/2090